EMMANUEL JOSEPH

The Palette of Resilience, Art as a Bridge Between Human Psychology and Environmental Crisis

Copyright © 2025 by Emmanuel Joseph

All rights reserved. No part of this publication may be reproduced, stored or transmitted in any form or by any means, electronic, mechanical, photocopying, recording, scanning, or otherwise without written permission from the publisher. It is illegal to copy this book, post it to a website, or distribute it by any other means without permission.

First edition

This book was professionally typeset on Reedsy.
Find out more at reedsy.com

Contents

1. Chapter 1: The Intersection of Art and Psychology — 1
2. Chapter 2: The Birth of Environmental Art — 2
3. Chapter 3: Art as a Tool for Healing — 3
4. Chapter 4: The Role of Art in Social Movements — 4
5. Chapter 5: Art and Environmental Resilience — 5
6. Chapter 6: The Power of Visual Storytelling — 6
7. Chapter 7: Art in Public Spaces — 7
8. Chapter 8: Art and Technology — 8
9. Chapter 9: Art Education and Environmental Awareness — 9
10. Chapter 10: The Future of Environmental Art — 10
11. Chapter 11: Personal Stories of Resilience — 11
12. Chapter 12: Conclusion: The Palette of Resilience — 12
13. Chapter 13: Art and Cultural Heritage — 13
14. Chapter 14: The Economics of Environmental Art — 14
15. Chapter 15: Art and Community Resilience — 15
16. Chapter 16: Art and Environmental Education — 16
17. Chapter 17: Art as a Catalyst for Innovation — 17
18. Chapter 18: Art and Environmental Activism — 18
19. Chapter 19: Art and Indigenous Knowledge — 19
20. Chapter 20: The Role of Art in Climate Change Communication — 20
21. Chapter 21: Art and Emotional Resilience — 21
22. Chapter 22: Art and the Anthropocene — 22

1

Chapter 1: The Intersection of Art and Psychology

Art has been a cornerstone of human expression for millennia, capturing the essence of emotions and experiences that words often fail to convey. From the cave paintings of Lascaux to modern digital creations, art has always been a medium for exploring the human psyche. In this chapter, we'll delve into the ways in which art serves as a mirror to our minds, reflecting our deepest fears, hopes, and dreams. We'll explore the psychological theories that explain why creating and experiencing art can be so profoundly therapeutic, and we'll meet artists who have used their work to navigate personal crises.

For instance, consider the story of Emma, a young woman who turned to painting as a way to cope with her anxiety. Emma found that the act of creating art allowed her to externalize her feelings and gain a sense of control over her emotions. Through her paintings, she was able to explore the root causes of her anxiety and develop healthier coping mechanisms. Her journey is a testament to the power of art to heal and transform.

2

Chapter 2: The Birth of Environmental Art

As humanity began to grapple with the impact of its actions on the planet, a new genre of art emerged: environmental art. This chapter traces the origins of environmental art, from the land art movement of the 1960s and 70s to contemporary eco-art. We'll explore how artists have used their work to raise awareness about environmental issues, create connections between people and nature, and inspire action. Through compelling stories and interviews, we'll see how environmental art has evolved and grown, becoming a powerful tool for advocacy and change.

One such artist is Andy Goldsworthy, whose ephemeral works created from natural materials highlight the transient beauty of nature and the impact of human activity. Goldsworthy's installations, often made from leaves, ice, stones, and branches, serve as meditations on the relationship between humans and the environment. His work invites viewers to consider their own interactions with nature and the ways in which they can contribute to its preservation.

3

Chapter 3: Art as a Tool for Healing

The connection between art and healing is well-documented, with countless studies showing the benefits of art therapy for mental health. In this chapter, we'll explore the science behind art therapy and its applications in treating trauma, depression, anxiety, and other psychological conditions. We'll hear from therapists and patients who have found solace and strength in the creative process, and we'll examine the ways in which art can help us process and overcome adversity. From community art projects to individual therapy sessions, we'll see how art can be a lifeline in times of crisis.

Consider the story of Daniel, a war veteran who struggled with PTSD. Through art therapy, Daniel found a way to express the intense emotions he had been carrying since returning from combat. His paintings, filled with bold colors and stark contrasts, became a way for him to process his experiences and regain a sense of peace. Daniel's story highlights the transformative power of art in the healing process.

Chapter 4: The Role of Art in Social Movements

Art has always played a vital role in social movements, from the suffragette posters of the early 20th century to the protest murals of the Black Lives Matter movement. In this chapter, we'll explore how artists have used their work to challenge injustice, amplify marginalized voices, and mobilize communities. Through powerful examples and personal stories, we'll see how art can be a catalyst for social change, sparking conversations and inspiring action. We'll also consider the ways in which artists can balance activism with self-care, using their work to sustain both themselves and their causes.

Take the example of the Guerrilla Girls, an anonymous group of feminist artists who use provocative posters and performances to challenge sexism and racism in the art world. Their work, often humorous and confrontational, has raised awareness about the lack of diversity in museums and galleries and has inspired a new generation of activist artists. The Guerrilla Girls' story demonstrates the power of art to bring attention to social issues and effect change.

5

Chapter 5: Art and Environmental Resilience

As the climate crisis continues to unfold, artists are finding new ways to address the challenges we face and foster resilience in their communities. This chapter examines how art can help us cope with environmental stressors, build adaptive capacities, and envision sustainable futures. We'll explore projects that combine art with science, technology, and traditional ecological knowledge, demonstrating the power of creative collaboration. We'll also hear from artists who are working on the frontlines of environmental crises, using their work to document, advocate, and inspire.

For example, consider the work of Maya Lin, the artist and architect behind the Vietnam Veterans Memorial in Washington, D.C. Lin has turned her attention to environmental issues with projects like "What Is Missing?"—a multi-sensory memorial to biodiversity loss. Through interactive installations and online platforms, Lin's work encourages viewers to reflect on the impact of human activity on the natural world and to take action to protect it.

Chapter 6: The Power of Visual Storytelling

Visual storytelling is a powerful tool for conveying complex ideas and emotions, and it has a unique ability to engage and inspire audiences. In this chapter, we'll explore the techniques and strategies that artists use to tell compelling visual stories, from composition and color theory to symbolism and metaphor. We'll examine case studies of artists who have effectively communicated their messages through visual storytelling, and we'll consider how these techniques can be applied to environmental issues. Through interviews and examples, we'll see how visual storytelling can make abstract concepts tangible and relatable.

One notable example is the work of photographer Sebastião Salgado, whose haunting images of environmental degradation and human suffering have raised awareness about the interconnectedness of social and environmental issues. Salgado's photographs, often stark and evocative, tell powerful stories that move viewers to consider their own roles in addressing these challenges. His work illustrates the potential of visual storytelling to drive change and inspire action.

7

Chapter 7: Art in Public Spaces

Public art has the power to transform spaces and create a sense of community, offering a shared experience that can foster connection and dialogue. In this chapter, we'll explore the impact of public art on communities and the environment, from large-scale installations to grassroots projects. We'll hear from artists and community members about the challenges and rewards of creating public art, and we'll consider the ways in which public art can address environmental and social issues. Through inspiring stories and examples, we'll see how public art can be a force for positive change.

For instance, the City Repair Project in Portland, Oregon, brings together artists, architects, and community members to create vibrant, sustainable public spaces. Through initiatives like intersection paintings, street furniture, and community gardens, the project aims to foster a sense of place and encourage environmental stewardship. The City Repair Project demonstrates how public art can transform urban environments and build stronger, more resilient communities.

8

Chapter 8: Art and Technology

The intersection of art and technology offers exciting possibilities for addressing environmental challenges and fostering resilience. In this chapter, we'll explore how artists are using cutting-edge technologies like virtual reality, augmented reality, and artificial intelligence to create immersive experiences and innovative solutions. We'll hear from artists and technologists about the potential and pitfalls of these collaborations, and we'll consider the ethical implications of using technology in art. Through case studies and interviews, we'll see how art and technology can work together to address complex problems and inspire new ways of thinking.

Consider the work of artists like Refik Anadol, who uses data and machine learning to create stunning visualizations of environmental data. Anadol's installations, which often involve large-scale projections and immersive environments, make abstract data tangible and engaging for viewers. By blending art and technology, Anadol's work helps raise awareness about environmental issues and encourages innovative solutions.

Chapter 9: Art Education and Environmental Awareness

Art education plays a crucial role in fostering environmental awareness and encouraging creative thinking. In this chapter, we'll examine the ways in which art education programs are integrating environmental themes and promoting sustainability. We'll hear from educators, students, and artists about the impact of these programs, and we'll consider the ways in which art can be used to teach critical thinking and problem-solving skills. Through inspiring stories and examples, we'll see how art education can empower the next generation of environmental stewards.

One example is the EcoArt program at a high school in California, where students create art projects that address environmental issues in their community. Through hands-on activities and interdisciplinary learning, students gain a deeper understanding of the connections between art, science, and the environment. The EcoArt program illustrates how art education can inspire young people to become active participants in environmental conservation and advocacy.

10

Chapter 10: The Future of Environmental Art

As we look to the future, environmental art will continue to evolve and adapt to the changing world. In this chapter, we'll explore emerging trends and new directions in environmental art, from eco-friendly materials and sustainable practices to interdisciplinary collaborations and global networks. We'll hear from artists and curators about their visions for the future, and we'll consider the ways in which environmental art can continue to inspire and effect change. Through forward-looking stories and examples, we'll see how environmental art can help us navigate the challenges of the 21st century.

Artists like Olafur Eliasson are leading the way with innovative projects that address climate change and sustainability. Eliasson's installations, which often involve large-scale, immersive experiences, aim to raise awareness about environmental issues and inspire action. His work, such as the "Ice Watch" installation featuring melting ice blocks from Greenland, encourages viewers to confront the realities of climate change and consider their roles in addressing it. Eliasson's vision for the future of environmental art highlights the potential for creativity to drive meaningful change.

11

Chapter 11: Personal Stories of Resilience

Art is deeply personal, and the stories of individual artists can offer powerful insights into the broader themes of resilience and environmental crisis. In this chapter, we'll hear from artists who have used their work to navigate personal and environmental challenges, finding strength and inspiration in the creative process.

Through interviews and personal narratives, we'll see how art can be a source of hope and resilience, helping individuals and communities to overcome adversity and envision a better future. We'll hear from artists like Sarah, who channeled her grief over losing her home in a wildfire into a series of powerful sculptures made from reclaimed materials. Her work not only helped her process her own trauma but also inspired others in her community to rebuild and find strength in the face of disaster. Sarah's story exemplifies the transformative power of art in times of crisis.

12

Chapter 12: Conclusion: The Palette of Resilience

In the final chapter, we'll reflect on the themes and stories explored throughout the book, considering the ways in which art can serve as a bridge between human psychology and environmental crisis. We'll synthesize the insights gained from artists, therapists, educators, and activists, and we'll consider the broader implications for our understanding of resilience and creativity. Through a compelling conclusion, we'll see how the palette of resilience can help us navigate the challenges of the modern world, finding strength and inspiration in the power of art.

Art has a unique ability to bring people together, foster empathy, and inspire action. As we face the unprecedented challenges of the 21st century, the lessons learned from art and the creative process can guide us in building a more resilient and sustainable future. By embracing the power of art to heal, connect, and transform, we can cultivate a deeper understanding of ourselves and our environment, ultimately creating a world where both people and the planet can thrive.

13

Chapter 13: Art and Cultural Heritage

Art is more than just individual expression; it serves as a repository of cultural heritage, preserving and transmitting the traditions, knowledge, and values of various communities. This chapter delves into the significance of art in maintaining cultural identity and continuity. We'll explore how artists around the world are using their work to celebrate and preserve their cultural heritage, ensuring that future generations can connect with their roots. Through captivating stories and examples, we'll see how art can bridge the gap between past and present, fostering a sense of identity and belonging.

One such story is that of the Aboriginal artist Emily Kame Kngwarreye, whose vibrant paintings are deeply rooted in her cultural heritage. Emily's work, characterized by bold patterns and colors, reflects the sacred traditions and landscapes of her people. Her art not only preserves the stories and knowledge of her community but also introduces these rich cultural narratives to a global audience. Emily's legacy highlights the power of art to celebrate and sustain cultural heritage.

14

Chapter 14: The Economics of Environmental Art

Creating and supporting environmental art often requires substantial resources, and understanding the economic dynamics behind it is crucial. This chapter examines the financial aspects of environmental art, including funding, patronage, and market influences. We'll hear from artists, curators, and funders about the challenges and opportunities they face in this field. By exploring case studies and interviews, we'll gain insights into the economic forces at play and consider how they shape the impact of environmental art.

Consider the story of Agnes Denes, a pioneer of environmental art known for her "Wheatfield - A Confrontation" project. In 1982, Agnes planted a two-acre wheatfield in downtown Manhattan, transforming a landfill into a lush, productive landscape. The project was funded by the Public Art Fund and highlighted the potential for urban agriculture. Agnes's work demonstrates how creative projects can attract funding and support while raising awareness about environmental issues.

15

Chapter 15: Art and Community Resilience

Art has the power to strengthen community bonds and foster resilience in the face of adversity. This chapter explores how art can bring people together, create shared experiences, and build social capital. We'll hear from community artists and organizers who use their work to address local challenges, from natural disasters to social injustice. Through inspiring stories and examples, we'll see how art can be a catalyst for community resilience and transformation.

For instance, the "Healing Through the Arts" program in New Orleans was initiated after Hurricane Katrina to help residents cope with trauma and rebuild their community. Through workshops, public murals, and collaborative projects, the program provided a platform for collective healing and expression. The art created through this initiative not only beautified the city but also fostered a sense of hope and unity among its residents. This example illustrates the profound impact that community art can have on resilience and recovery.

16

Chapter 16: Art and Environmental Education

Environmental education is essential for fostering a deeper understanding of the natural world and inspiring sustainable behavior. This chapter examines the role of art in environmental education, from school programs to public campaigns. We'll hear from educators, students, and artists about the impact of integrating art into environmental education and consider how creative approaches can enhance learning and engagement. Through case studies and examples, we'll see how art can be an effective tool for environmental education.

One notable example is the "Art and Ecology" program at the Sierra Nevada Field Campus, where students create art projects that explore ecological themes. Through fieldwork and hands-on activities, students learn about local ecosystems and environmental issues while developing their artistic skills. The program demonstrates how art can deepen environmental understanding and inspire a sense of stewardship in participants.

17

Chapter 17: Art as a Catalyst for Innovation

Art has always been a source of innovation, pushing the boundaries of creativity and inspiring new ways of thinking. This chapter explores how art can drive innovation in addressing environmental challenges. We'll hear from artists, scientists, and technologists who are collaborating to develop innovative solutions, and we'll consider the role of creativity in problem-solving. Through inspiring stories and examples, we'll see how art can be a catalyst for innovation and a powerful force for change.

Take the work of Studio Roosegaarde, a design lab that merges art, technology, and environmental sustainability. Their projects, such as the "Smog Free Tower" and "Waterlicht," use innovative design to address issues like air pollution and rising sea levels. By combining artistic vision with cutting-edge technology, Studio Roosegaarde's work demonstrates the potential for creative solutions to address complex environmental problems.

18

Chapter 18: Art and Environmental Activism

Art has long been a powerful tool for activism, amplifying voices and galvanizing movements. In this chapter, we'll explore how artists are using their work to address environmental issues and inspire change. We'll hear from activists who incorporate art into their campaigns, creating visual statements that capture attention and evoke emotion. By examining case studies and interviews, we'll see how art can turn abstract environmental concepts into compelling narratives that drive action.

Consider the work of Banksy, the elusive street artist known for his provocative and politically charged pieces. Banksy's artwork often highlights social and environmental issues, such as climate change and deforestation. His piece "Season's Greetings," featuring a child catching ash from a dumpster fire as though it were snow, starkly comments on air pollution. Banksy's ability to merge art with activism demonstrates the potential of creative expression to influence public perception and encourage environmental stewardship.

19

Chapter 19: Art and Indigenous Knowledge

Indigenous communities have a profound connection to their environments, and their art often reflects deep ecological knowledge and sustainable practices. This chapter will explore how indigenous artists use their work to convey traditional ecological wisdom and advocate for environmental conservation. We'll hear from indigenous artists about the role of art in preserving cultural heritage and promoting sustainable living. Through compelling stories and examples, we'll see how indigenous art can serve as a bridge between ancient wisdom and contemporary environmental challenges.

One such artist is Tlingit carver and storyteller Wayne Price, who uses traditional carving techniques to create totem poles that tell the stories of his people and their relationship with the land. Wayne's work not only preserves cultural traditions but also raises awareness about the importance of environmental stewardship. His art serves as a reminder of the deep connections between culture, identity, and the natural world.

Chapter 20: The Role of Art in Climate Change Communication

Climate change is a complex and often overwhelming issue, but art can play a crucial role in making it more accessible and engaging. This chapter will explore how artists are using their work to communicate the science and impacts of climate change, making the issue more relatable and urgent for audiences. We'll hear from artists and scientists who collaborate to create visual and experiential representations of climate data. Through case studies and examples, we'll see how art can translate complex information into compelling stories that inspire action.

Consider the work of artist and climate activist Zaria Forman, whose large-scale pastel drawings depict the melting icebergs and rising seas caused by climate change. Zaria's stunningly realistic art captures the beauty and fragility of the natural world, creating an emotional connection that motivates viewers to care about and take action on climate issues. Her work exemplifies the power of art to communicate the urgency of climate change in a visually and emotionally impactful way.

Chapter 21: Art and Emotional Resilience

The emotional toll of environmental crises can be significant, leading to feelings of grief, anxiety, and helplessness. In this chapter, we'll explore how art can help individuals and communities build emotional resilience in the face of these challenges. We'll hear from artists, therapists, and community leaders who use art to process and express emotions related to environmental stress. Through personal stories and therapeutic practices, we'll see how creative expression can foster hope, connection, and healing.

For example, the "Climate Grief" project, initiated by artist and therapist Amy Comparetto, provides a space for individuals to express their emotions about climate change through art. Participants create visual representations of their feelings, which are then shared in community exhibits and discussions. The project aims to validate and process the complex emotions associated with climate change, fostering a sense of solidarity and resilience. Amy's work highlights the therapeutic potential of art in addressing the emotional aspects of environmental crises.

22

Chapter 22: Art and the Anthropocene

The Anthropocene, the current geological epoch characterized by significant human impact on the Earth, presents unique challenges and opportunities for artists. In this chapter, we'll explore how artists are grappling with the themes of the Anthropocene, creating work that reflects the profound changes occurring in our world. We'll hear from artists who use their work to critique human activities, celebrate resilience, and imagine new futures. Through compelling stories and examples, we'll see how art can help us navigate the complexities of living in the Anthropocene.

One such artist is Olafur Eliasson, known for his large-scale installations that explore the relationship between humans and the environment. His project "The Weather Project," installed at the Tate Modern in London, created an immersive experience that invited viewers to reflect on their connection to the natural world. Eliasson's work encourages contemplation of our role in shaping the Earth's future and the potential for collective action.

The Palette of Resilience: Art as a Bridge Between Human Psychology and Environmental Crisis is a compelling exploration of the transformative power of art. Spanning seventeen thought-provoking chapters, this book delves into the myriad ways art intersects with human psychology and the ongoing environmental crisis. From the therapeutic benefits of creating and experiencing art to the role of environmental art in raising awareness

CHAPTER 22: ART AND THE ANTHROPOCENE

and inspiring action, this book offers a rich tapestry of stories, insights, and examples.

You'll journey through the origins of environmental art, the science behind art therapy, the role of art in social movements, and the impact of public art on communities and the environment. The book also explores the intersection of art and technology, the importance of art education, and the future of environmental art. Personal stories of resilience and innovation further illustrate the profound impact art can have on individuals and communities.

This book is not just a collection of essays but a vibrant celebration of creativity, resilience, and hope. Whether you're an artist, an environmental advocate, or simply someone looking for inspiration, **The Palette of Resilience** will open your eyes to the incredible potential of art to heal, connect, and transform our world.

www.ingramcontent.com/pod-product-compliance
Lightning Source LLC
LaVergne TN
LVHW020508080526
838202LV00057B/6242